St Trinian's Chapel

CASTLES AND
OLD CHURCHES OF
THE ISLE OF MAN

Mike Salter

FOLLY PUBLICATIONS

ACKNOWLEDGEMENTS

The photographs in this book were all taken by the author, who also prepared the plans, drawings, and the map showing the positions of the various monuments that are described. Most of the plans are at a common scale of 1:400 but the plans of Castle Rushen and Derby Fort are at 1:800 and that showing all the buildings on St Patrick's Isle at Peel is at 1:1250. Thanks are due to Nadine and Jimmy of Ballabrooie, near St Johns, in whose orchard the author camped in July 1996. Thanks also to Max Barfield of Hyde in Cheshire for the loan of a camera, transport to and from the ferryports in England, and for the use of the computer on which part of the text was prepared, and to my mother Marjorie Salter, who checked through the text.

ABOUT THIS BOOK

This book is the 17th in a series now describing castles and pre 19th century churches throughout all of Wales and Scotland and much of the rest of Britain. Normally the series (see inside back cover) features different volumes for castles and churches for each area. Because of the comparatively small number of ancient buildings on the Isle of Man, the cathedral, the bishop's fortified house, two earthworks, two stone castles, several 16th and 17th century artillery forts, twenty parish churches and their contents up to the early 19th century, a number of other chapels, and the sites of four religious houses have here been put together to produce a book of suitable length.

It is intended that visitors, particularly those wanting to visit the elusive keeills, should use sheet 95 in the Ordnance Survey Landranger 1:50,000 series. The two letters and six digits which appear after the names of the buildings are Ordnance Survey grid references. The map contains instructions on how these are worked out.

ACCESS TO THE BUILDINGS

All the parish churches are accessible and most of them are kept open during the day. Many of the keeill sites lie on private land but public paths lead to Balladoole, Lag Ny Keeilley, and Spooyt Vane and the three in the graveyard at Maughold are freely accessible. There is also free access to Ballachurry Fort, The Broogh, the battery site at Gob ny rona, and the exteriors of the chapel and fort on St Michael's Island, Derby Haven, and St Trinian's Chapel. An admission fee is payable for access to the interiors of Castle Rushen and the castle and cathedral at Peel. Bishopscourt, Cronk Howe Mooar, and Rushen Abbey can be seen from nearby public roads.

ABOUT THE AUTHOR

Mike Salter is 43 and has been a professional writer and publisher since he went on the Government Enterprise Allowance Scheme for unemployed people in 1988. He is particularly interested in the planning and layout of medieval buildings and has a huge collection of plans of churches and castles he has measured during tours (mostly by bicycle and motorcycle) throughout all parts of the British Isles since 1968. Wolverhampton born and bred, Mike now lives in an old cottage beside the Malvern Hills. His other interests include walking, railways, board games, morris dancing, and playing percussion and calling dances with a folk group.

Copyright 1997 Mike Salter.   First published March 1997
Folly Publications, Folly Cottage, 151 West Malvern Rd, Malvern, Worcs, WR14 4AY
Printed by Aspect Design, 89 Newtown Rd, Malvern, Worcs, WR14 2PD

St George's Church, Douglas

CONTENTS

Introduction	Page	4
Glossary of Terms	Page	8
Further Reading	Page	8
Bishopscourt	Page	9
Castle Rushen	Page	10
Peel Castle and Cathedral	Page	16
Artillery Forts	Page	28
Religious Houses	Page	30
Gazetteer of Parish Churches	Page	32

INTRODUCTION

Christianity was introduced to the Isle of Man in the 5th or 6th century and resulted in the construction in huge numbers of tiny chapels called keeills. The earliest ones were perhaps built of earth or wattle and daub with thatched roofs. Over 180 examples with drystone walls dating from probably the 8th to the 12th centuries are known to have existed although there are now only remains of about 40 of them. In some cases they occur in groups, and at Maughold three survive and a fourth is known. Few of them are more than 6m long or 3.5m wide or have walling more than 1m high. Some appear to have earth walls with a drystone inner face. Normally the only feature to remain is a west doorway, although some have traces of an altar.

The Isle of Man has a superb collection of about 180 cross-slabs dating from c650 to 1150. A number are kept in the Manx Museum in Douglas and the remainder are to be found at thirteen of the churches. Maughold was an important Celtic monastic site and has the best collection of early slabs up to c800 with simple compass-arc decoration, plus larger 9th century examples with ring headed crosses in low relief and background decoration. Other selections of note are at Lonan Old Church and Onchan. The finest of the Celtic slabs is a crucifixion scene found in 1773 in a keeill on the Calf of Man, and now in the Museum. Pagan Norsemen began to settle in Man in the late 9th century but by the 10th century their descendants seem to have adopted Christianity. Cross slabs of the 10th and 11th centuries abound and often combine traditional Celtic art forms with figures and animals sometimes illustrating pagan Norse myths. Many of the slabs have runic inscriptions with names and other useful information. Collections of this period are at Andreas, Michael, Maughold, and Braddan, which also has two pillar crosses. Of the 10th century is the round tower on St Patrick's Isle at Peel. It combined the functions of a treasury, lookout point, and refuge and is shorter version of those found at early monastic sites in Ireland. Near it is a church of the same period, originally with antae, but rebuilt in the 12th century with herring-bone masonry of the type associated with the late Saxon and early Norman periods in England.

North Keeill at Maughold

Keeill at Lag ny Keeilley

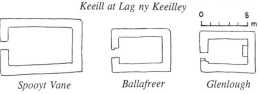

0   5
L_l_l_l_l_l m

Spooyt Vane   *Ballafreer*   *Glenlough*

Plans of Keeills   *Cross-slabs at Maughold*

A dynasty of Norse kings of Man and the Western Isles of Scotland existed in the 10th century but was only securely established after Godred I's victory at Skyhill in 1079. The kings of Norway tried to assert an overlordship and from 1098 until he was killed in Ulster in 1103, Magnus Barelegs ruled Man directly. He imported timber for the building of three forts. It is assumed that one lay on St Patrick's Island at Peel and that the typically Norman castle mound at Cronk Howe Mooar (SC 205697) may have been another. It is possible that the third was at The Broogh (SC 318741), but the earthwork there is probably earlier. Cronk Howe Mooar is a natural mound rising 9m above the surrounding ditch and lies in a flat marshy position. Drystone walling has been noted on the depressed summit 20m long by 12m wide. There are two causeways across the ditch and a low mound beyond to the east which appears to be natural but could be part of a bailey rampart. The Broogh has a mound 3m high and 20m across on the sloping top with two concentric surrounding ditches.

Cronk Howe Mooar

Cross at Maughold

Former chapel of St Mary at Castletown

The Norse kings' original principal seat seems to have been at Peel, the administrative centre for the northern half of the island. The centre for the southern half was at Castletown where a stone keep was built in the late 12th century. It was about this time that the seventeen parishes of the island were established, each with a parish church, although supplemented by chapels of ease as needed. Throughout the medieval period and beyond the parish churches retained their simple rectangular form with neither separate chancels or side aisles. The cruciform 13th century cathedral at Peel and the 12th century Cistercian abbey church at Rushen both had aisles and towers but these do not occur in the parish churches although there were once medieval towers at Andreas and Michael. The small chapel at Castletown has an arcade of a former south aisle. No late medieval windows survive complete with tracery in any of the churches, not even the cathedral, but there is a complete 12th century chapel at St Michael's, other Norman windows at St Trinian's chapel, and 13th century lancets survive at Maughold, Lonan Old Church, and the cathedral, where there are also cusped lancets and a two light west window. Maughold has a late medieval pillar cross now taken inside the church to help preserve it.

The defeat of King Haakon of Norway in 1263 at Largs culminated in Man and the Western Isles being ceded in 1266 to Alexander III of Scotland. After Alexander's infant daughter Margaret died in 1290 the English Crown took an increasing interest in the strategically important Isle of Man. It became subject to Scottish raids and in 1313 Robert Bruce captured and destroyed Castle Rushen. English overlordship was finally secured in 1333 when Edward III installed the Montague Earls of Salisbury as Kings of Man. By the 1380s the bishops had built a fortified tower at Bishopscourt as their residence whilst the Montagues had rebuilt Castle Rushen in a suitable form to make it their chief residence and administration centre on the island. The Kings of Man had transferred there in the 1230s if not before, and handed St Patrick's Island at Peel over to the church. However, that site was too exposed to raids and too obvious a site for a fortress to remain purely an ecclesiastical centre. It was refortified in the 1390s by William Scrope, Earl of Wiltshire, and again in the 1460s by Lord Stanley, whose great-grandfather was created King of Man by Henry IV in 1405.

Castle Rushen

Thomas Stanley, 2nd Earl of Derby in the reign of Henry VIII, found it tactful to style himself Lords of Man, claiming that it was better to be a great lord than a petty king. In the 1540s his son Edward, 3rd Earl, provided Castle Rushen with an outer line of defence by and against cannon, and circular artillery forts were also built at Douglas, Peel, and Derbyhaven. The 7th Earl was on Man from 1744 until 1651 and fortified the island against the English Parliament. A rectangular earth fort with diamond shaped corner bastions in the latest fashion was built at Ballachurry to control the north end of the island, and batteries were built to cover landing places at Ramsey, Derbyhaven and Peel. The batteries were refortified in the 1690s when there was a risk of raids by privateers. The accommodation at Castle Rushen was improved in the 1590s, and that at Peel in the early and late 17th centuries. Both castles remained in use as residences, fortresses and administrative centres until the early 18th century. Peel then became ruinous although still occasionally garrisoned and armed with artillery until 1870, whilst Castle Rushen remained a centre of government until the 20th century and was a prison throughout the 19th century. There was no resident Lord of Man after the island passed in 1736 to James, 2nd Duke of Atholl. In 1764, under the Act of Revestment, the 3rd Duke surrendered Man to the British government, and the British Crown has appointed governors ever since.

The cathedral was gradually allowed to fall into ruin during the 18th century but there was much rebuilding in the parish churches. Of that period is much of the fabric at Arbory, Ballaugh Old Church, Marown Old Church, and Braddan, where a tower was added. An entirely new church of some size with an aisled nave and a west tower was built at Douglas in the 1780s. There was another wave of rebuilding in the late 19th century and many of the parish churches are mostly or entirely of that date.

Derby Fort

GLOSSARY OF TERMS

Ashlar	- Masonry of blocks with even faces and square edges.
Bailey	- A defensible space enclosed by a wall or palisade and a ditch.
Barbican	- A building or enclosure defending a castle entrance.
Bastion	- A squat projecting tower rising no higher than the curtain wall.
Bartizan	- A turret corbelled out from a wall, usually at the summit.
Batter	- An inward inclination of a wall face.
Chancel	- The eastern part of a church used by the clery.
Corbel	- A projecting bracket supporting other stonework or timbers.
Culverin	- Cannon 9ft-11ft long, firing an 18lb ball about 5.5" in diameter.
Curtain Wall	- A high enclosing stone wall around a bailey.
Embattled	- Provided with a parapet with indentations (crenellations).
Glacis	- Long slope extending down and out from a defensive circuit. .
Keeill	- A small chapel of the Early Christian period.
Keep	- A citadel or ultimate strongpoint. Originally called a donjon.
Lancet	- A long and comparatively narrow window with a pointed head.
Light	- A compartment of a window.
Merlons	- The upstanding portions of a crenellated parapet.
Minion	- Cannon about 6.5ft long, firing 5lb ball about 3.25" in diameter.
Moat	- A ditch, water filled or dry, around an enclosure.
Motte	- A steeply sided flat topped mound, usually mostly man-made.
Nave	- The part of a church used by the congregation.
Ogham	- A type of script using notches cut over an edge on a stone
Parapet	- A wall for protection at any sudden drop.
Pilaster	- A buttress of little projection although it may be quite wide.
Piscina	- A stone basin used for washing out holy vessels after mass.
Plinth	- The projecting base of a wall. It may be battered or stepped.
Portcullis	- A wooden gate designed to rise and fall in vertical grooves.
Postern	- A secondary gateway or doorway. A back entrance.
Saker	- Cannon 6ft-8ft long, firing a 6lb ball about 3.5" in diameter.
Scale-and-Platt Stair	- Staircase with short straight flights and turns at landings.
Transept	- A projecting body. Used in pairs to make a church cruciform.
Trefoiled	- Divided into three lobes by cusps.
Wall-walk	- A walkway on top of a wall, protected by a parapet.
Ward	- A stone walled defensive enclosure.

FURTHER READING

Ancient Centres of Government of the Isle of Man, Robert Curphey
The Ancient & Historic Monuments of the Isle of Man, Manx Museum, 1973
The Art of the Manx Crosses, A.M.Cubbon, Manx Museum, 1983
Portrait of the Isle of Man, E.H.Stenning, 3rd edition 1975
The Peel Castle Dig, David Freke, Manx Museum, 1995
Peel Castle Official Guide, David Craine, 1980
Manx Crosses, P.M.C Kermode, 1907
Journal of the Manx Museum, particularly Vol VII (artillery batteries to 1765)
Isle of Man Natural History and Antiquarian Society annual transactions.
Pamphlets are available at the following churches: Ballaugh, Braddan,
    Bride, Douglas, Lezayre, Marown, Maughold, Michael, Santan.

Bishopscourt from the south

BISHOPSCOURT   SC 328924

Simon, Bishop of Sodor is said to have died here in 1247, and the place is mentioned as held by the bishops in a Papal Bull of 1231, but the tower house forming the core of a mansion long used by the bishops is more likely to be of the time of Bishop Duncan (1374-92). Originally probably of three storeys, it now contains four levels of rooms each with a pair of large modern windows facing SE towards the main road. The range to the west is a 15th or 16th century hall block but again much remodelled. The house was occupied by Parliamentary commissioners in the 1650s and was much repaired c1700 by Bishop Wilson, who laid out the grounds. The house lies in the parish of Michael whilst the chapel of St Nicholas immediately to the east lies in the parish of Ballaugh. Bishop Crigan built a new chapel c1790 on the site of the late medieval one and Bishop Powys in the 1850s added transepts. By the house are remains of a mid 17th century earthwork fort with corner bastions.

Bishopscourt from the east

CASTLE RUSHEN   SC 265674

A tower 17m square over rough rubble walls up to 2.5m thick was erected here in the late 12th century either by Godred II in the period 1164 to 1187, or his successor Reginald I, who ruled the Island of Man until ousted by his brother Olaf in 1226 and finally defeated and killed in 1228. It probably contained three storeys forming a storage basement, hall, and lord's bedroom respectively and seems to have been entered at hall level through a forebuilding on the north side. Only the featureless lower parts now survive of this tower as first built and of the towers or wings roughly 6.5m square added later against the middle of the south and east sides perhaps by Harold I in the 1240s or Magnus in the 1250s. The original upper parts are assumed to have been destroyed by Robert Bruce after he captured Castle Rushen in June 1313 after a three week siege, the slighting of castles he could not hold being his usual policy. From at least the 1230s it appears that the tower formed the principal residence and administration centre seat of the kings and it must have been accompanied by numerous timber outbuildings within a palisade and ditch.

After he became King of Man in 1333, William Montague, Earl of Salisbury commenced rebuilding the keep. A battered plinth was erected against the stump of the old walls and then they were continued upward with fine dressed limestone blocks. A tower was added on the east side to match those on the south and west and the forebuilding on the north side was replaced by a fine twin-towered gatehouse. The NE corner of the interior was left open as a court and narrow ranges containing lordly apartments were built on the south and west sides. Under William, 2nd Earl of Salisbury, who succeeded his father in 1344 and lived intil 1393, work on the castle continued, the keep being completed with its gatehouse and flanking towers rising one stage higher than the main battlements. A curtain wall over 2m thick was then built around the keep to enclose a nine sided court 49m wide from east to west by 54m long, entered through its own gatehouse.

Castle Rushen from the east

Bartizans on the curtain wall at Castle Rushen

Throughout the 15th century the castle was found to be adequate as a residence and fortress by the Stanleys, but the development of cannon necessitated a strengthening of the defences by Edward Stanley, 3rd Earl of Derby, in the 1540s. The recently dissolved Rushen Abbey probably provided a convenient source of materials. A glacis with an outer face sloping down to ground level was built around the outer edge of the moat to deflect cannon balls away from the curtain wall. The glacis was flanked by three towers designed to carry cannon. Those on the east and SW, which were D-shaped, were destroyed in the late 18th and early 19th century respectively. A square postern turret adjoined the SW tower. The more modestly sized north tower, a full round 10m in diameter, now alone survives. Originally it had guns both at ground level and on a flat roof, but a conical roof, now mostly collapsed, was provided in the late 16th century. A stair rises in the thickness of the wall from the entrance on the south side up to a top storey with a fireplace. In later years this tower served as a dovecote.

In 1580-3 Henry, 4th Earl of Derby erected a new domestic block now called Derby House on the NE side of the courtyard. At the same time the barbican was extended, an eight gun battery was erected by the water's edge north of the entrance, and a three storey building containing a chapel with a stable below was put up beside the access ramp to the keep. Derby House was given a third storey in 1644 and the Earl and Countess used it as their main residence until 1651. In that year the Earl was captured at Worcester after Charles II's defeat there, and executed at Bolton. The Countess moved into the keep and prepared for a siege. In the event this was brief because the garrison became demoralised after Colonel Dukinfield set up his siege guns against the castle. Some of defenders descended the walls and opened the postern at the SW corner, giving access to the glacis and making defence of the curtain difficult. Agreement was then reached for a surrender allowing the garrison to go free and the Countess and her family to return to England to make their peace with Parliament. Among the equipment then found within the castle upon its surrender were four crossbows. Another inventory of munitions here in 1701 mentions 20 battleaxes, 11 flintlocks, 5 harquebusses, and 28 matchlocks.

The moat at Castle Rushen

William, 9th Earl of Derby refurnished Derby House in the 1670s but the castle had by now little military purpose and the other buildings were allowed to decay and the few cannon were only used for firing salutes. Most of the rooms in the keep were roofless by 1788, although the two guardrooms were still in use as a prison and debtors were confined in the porter's lodge in the outer gate and in the curtain wall towers. In the early 19th century the keep was repaired and remodelled in an attempt to create more up to date prison accommodation and the surrounding court was divided in three to give separate exercise yards for male and female prisoners and debtors. The chapel became the Gaoler's office and the top room of the gatehouse became a courtroom. A Home Office report in 1885 found the castle "incurably defective" as a gaol, and it ceased to be used as such after a new prison was opened at Douglas in 1891. For a while the castle continued to have some administrative function but it was carefully restored c1910 to remove most of the 19th century alterations, and has since been an ancient monument.

The castle is entered through a gateway with two round flanking turrets in an outer barbican added in the 16th century and heightened in 1644. The passage, commanded by the curtain wall-walk on one side and a high wall mostly of late 14th century date on the other, leads to an arch on the east side of the outer gatehouse where there was a drawbridge over a pit. A passage over the arch allowed access from the curtain wall-walk to a pair of latrines on the inner barbican outer wall. The outer gatehouse, or Burn Tower, measures 14m by 15m and has a very unusual internal layout. The SE corner forms the entrance passage, making a right angled turn through the building, leaving rooms for porters and guards on the NE and the west. Below is a large vaulted cellar into which stores were hoisted through a hatch from the entrance passage. Above is a room once used by the castle governor but later used by the Courts of Chancery and exchequer, and the meeting place of the Keys until 1710. Modern toilets are accommodated in a 19th century block along the south side of the outer barbican.

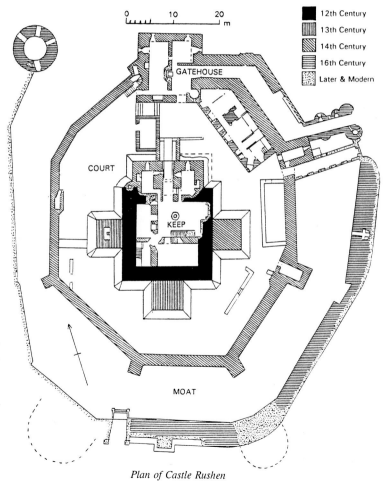

Plan of Castle Rushen

The curtain wall-walk is reached by an open stair against the west side of the outer gatehouse. The curtain has nine sides but effectively forms an elongated octogon with the NW corner cut off by a short extra side terminated at either end by a square bartizan. The next corner, facing SW, has a buttress able to support a corbelled fighting top of greater projection than the bartizans. The two corners facing the town square to the south have slightly larger buttresses carrying tiny rooms in caphouses upon moulded corbelling (see front cover). The turrets at the two eastern corners are wide enough (about 5m) to contain store rooms at courtyard level and higher up (reached by ladders) as well as larger rooms in their corbelled out top storeys. The curtain wall-walk passes by all four of these upper rooms on the east and south corners, which were used by the officers of the garrison, and once continued past the topmost storey of Derby House to the inner barbican and outer gatehouse. The addition of the top storey of Derby House in 1644 provided space for bedrooms for the earl and countess, a closet, a dressing room and a wardrobe. Access to them is by a stair in the SE corner. South of Derby House are foundations of a kitchen against the curtain. Slighter remnants further south lie where a smithy is marked on a mid 18th century plan. There is a well beside the keep here and another alongside Derby House.

Upper part of the inner gatehouse

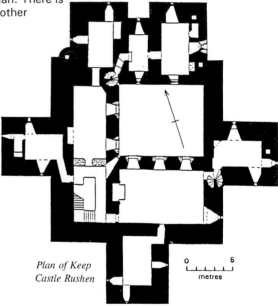

Plan of Keep
Castle Rushen

0   5
metres

Castle Rushen

The court inside the keep at Castle Rushen

The inner gatehouse was reached across a turning bridge. The passage was closed by two portcullises and a two-leaved door. There are guard rooms on either side, that to the east being the alleged prison of Bishop Wilson. Trap-doors in the floors of these rooms give access to stores or prisons below. A spiral stair on the inner side of the western gatehouse tower gives access to rooms on four upper levels. Each level contains a room in each tower and a small room in between except for the topmost level forming one big room with nine windows. Probably this room was used for the storage and copying of charters originally, but it was later used as a courtroom. One room in the west tower on the fourth of the six storeys is only accessible from the lord's room in the west range and was presumably a treasury.

The small court in the keep contains a well in the middle. An arch in the east wall is all that remains of a small range which once stood on that side. A long flight of steps leads up to two doorways at the NE corner of the south range. One leads into a kitchen in the east tower and the other into the service end of the main hall, a room 9.5m long by 5.5m wide. A spiral leads off beside the hall doorway to another, more private, hall for the lord above and then to the main wall-walk. The upper hall has a fireplace in the west wall, three north windows facing the court, and one narrow east window which is the only medieval opening in the outer wall of the main block. The south range is 3.6m wide inside and is now divided at each level into a room with windows facing east into the court, and a well for a scale-and-platt staircase tucked into the dark SW corner. How the range was originally laid out is uncertain. As with the south range, the lowest level is a store, and then there are two upper levels of private rooms, the lower having a fireplace on the east side and the upper having a fireplace on the west. The south and west towers contain private rooms corresponding to these upper levels, the lowest rooms in each case having two window embrasures with seats and being covered by a ribbed vault. The rooms in the west tower have latrines contained in its west end wall. The three towers rise one stage above the main wall-walk, at which level the south tower contains what was once the chapel of St Katherine, but which now contains a clock mechanism.

PEEL CASTLE AND CATHEDRAL   SC 242846

St Patrick's Island at Peel was occupied by a monastery during the so-called Dark Ages. Excavations in 1982-7 found evidence of Christian burials of the 7th or 8th century with a few 10th century pagan burials overlying them. The earliest part of the church of St Patrick and the round tower standing west of it are probably 10th century and an altar stone of that period was found during an excavation in 1962. The 1980s excavation revealed foundations of a keeill or tiny chapel of about the same early period beyond the north wall of the cathedral chancel. The excavations also revealed traces of a drystone rampart in the same area, possibly a relic of a fort which Magnus Barelegs, King of Norway is assumed to established here during his rule over Man from 1198 to 1103. Another excavation discovery was a building of unknown usage but evident importance from the standard of its construction. It was of wood with thin stone walling forming the base of the walls. The floor was originally suspended but was later replaced by stone slabs and then by a layer of clay and mortar. It is tempting to associate this structure with the residence and centre of government that the Manx kings had on St Patrick's Isle until they transferred their seat to Castle Rushen and in 1257 King Mugnus formally handed over the isle to the church. Two of the kings died here, Godred II in 1187, and Olaf II in 1237. Olaf had driven his brother Reginald I from the throne in 1226 but the latter, a noted seafarer, made a successful attack on Olaf's fleet lying at anchor in the harbour at Peel in 1228, only to be defeated and killed in a battle at Tynwald.

Simon, Abbot of Iona, d1247, became Bishop of Sodor c1225 and is credited with the building of the chancel of the cathedral. The excavations of the 1980s showed that at about the same time a stone hall block orientated east-west was erected north of it. Tests on a fireplace in the hall showed that it remained in use until the late 14th century. Beyond it, and orientated north-south, was an apartment block 15m long by 6m wide, and beyond that a detached kitchen with an oven projecting from its north wall. These buildings were probably used as a residence by the bishop himself.

Peel Castle and Cathedral from the SE

Peel Castle from Peel Hill

St Patrick's Island was too useful as a potential fortress during the quarrels between the Scots and English crowns over possession of Man for it to be left in peace as a purely religious site. The 1980s excavations found that above the Norse rampart facing the harbour north of the cathedral there were remains of an earth rampart probably built soon after the English regained control of the Isle of Man in 1333. It is from the wooden palisade or "peel" surmounting this rampart that the castle eventually took its name. There was a conflict of interest between the garrison and the clergy, and in 1365 there is a record of the bishop trying in vain to recover "his cathedral church and precincts" then occupied by troops installed by the Montague family. The buildings were devastated by a Scottish raid in 1388. On becoming Lord of Man in 1393 Sir William le Scrope applied to the Pope for a "Licence to build a castle in the place commonly called Patrykysholm, near and belonging to the church of Sodor situate in his kingdom, whose buildings have been destroyed by the invasion of his enemies of the kingdom and cannot, through the slenderness of its means, be repaired, whereby divine worship has been almost utterly diminished and divine offices have for a long time not been celebrated. He intends to repair the church to which the castle will serve as a defence".

Scrope re-roofed and embattled the cathedral, erected new apartments to serve a college of priests on the site of the 13th century domestic buildings, and built the existing gatehouse and adjacent walls, plus several other towers around the island. Much of the circuit remained enclosed only by a palisade until the curtain wall was built by Thomas, Lord Stanley probably in the 1460s as a defence against the Scots. Excavations have shown that what was previously thought to be an earlier rampart against the curtain is in fact of the same period, although it was widened on the north side to take cannon in the 16th century. The round battery overlooking the harbour entrance outside the curtain and the Half Moon Battery west of the cathedral are assumed to have been built by Edward, 3rd Earl of Derby, as a response to a Scottish raid in 1547. A threat of invasion by the Spanish prompted the strengthening of Peel castle in 1593 by Ferdinando, 5th Earl of Derby, and the installation of a garrison of 36 men. When the earl died suddenly in 1594 Queen Elizabeth took control of Man, installing a governor, Sir Thomas Gerrard who was ordered "to consider the best means of defence, as the forts are but meanly provided". The armoury and hall near St Patrick's church are of about this time.

The Cathedral and Half Moon Battery, Peel

The Stanley Earls of Derby were staunch catholics and thus not in any hurry to eject the clery as happened in other colleges in England. However after the Isle of Man was returned by James I to the 6th Earl, the latter took over the clerical apartments at Peel and remodelled them as a residence for himself. In 1643 James, 7th Earl of Derby, managed to stave off a revolt by the Manx people against his unpopular rule by holding a meeting of the Council, Keys and people at Creg Malin Green within sight of Peel Castle. At this meeting he had seized the Manx popular leader Edward Christian, a former Deputy Governor, and had him imprisoned in the castle. The Earl occupied Man in the Royalist cause from 1644 to 1651 and had the defences at Peel strengthened. Of this period are the walls running east and south of the Half Moon Battery provided to act as an additional line of defence should the main gate be forced, the earthworks around the central Dyall Mound, and the loopholed walls connecting the harbour battery to the main curtain and those projecting north of Fenella's Tower, both sets greatly aiding flanking fire on the north side. Slight traces remain of a battery on Peel Hill built in 1648 to command the crossing point to the castle across the harbour. When the castle surrendered to Colonel Duckenfield in 1651 it contained 24 cannon and many rich furnishings in the apartments. The prisoner Edward Christian was then finally released but was reincarcerated in 1660 and died within the walls the following year.

The Stanleys continued to make much use of Peel Castle as a residence in the late 17th century, the apartments being remodelled in the 1660s by Charles, 8th Earl, with further work later carried out for William, 9th Earl. The length of curtain wall which originally passed in front of the east end of the cathedral and the ground on which it stood collapsed in this period, and in 1683 it was recommended that doors be opened in the chancel side walls to allow the watchmen to pass through. There were then 18 guns mounted at the castle which were used in 1692 to prevent an attempt by a privateeer to capture three colliers which had "run themselves under his lordship's castle of Peel". In 1713 there were 15 guns, most of which faced out to sea. The causeway connecting St Patrick's Island to the mainland was erected in the 1750s. The Duke of Atholl ordered the castle to be dismantled except for the armoury and storehouse, the garrison were paid off, and at the Revestment of 1765 the best of the guns were removed to his seat at Blair Castle in Perthshire.

St Patrick's Church, Peel

The deterioration of the cathedral began during the period 1643 to 1661 when there was no bishop. It was "in ruins" in 1662 but was re-roofed in the 1690s. Bishop Wilson then clashed with the island governor, who refused access to the cathedral, even for services, let alone maintenance, and in the 1730s the roofs from the nave and transepts were removed for re-use on a new stable block being erected at Castletown. The chancel roof was repaired when Bishop Hildesley was installed in 1755, and it was still sufficiently watertight to allow the installation of Bishop Crigan in 1784, but by 1824 the whole building was roofless, and despite later proposals for restoration, so it has remained. Prints of the 1770s show that the lord's apartments, which were empty but intact in the 1730s, had become ruined. Problems with privateers during the American War of Independance led to the mounting of four guns in the castle in 1782, probably on the same site as that used for the mounting of two 18 pounder guns from 1816 until 1822. The island was last used by the military when a naval reserve battery of two 32 pounders was mounted upon it from 1861 until 1870. Around that time the then ruinous curtain wall was repaired and the castle opened to the public as an ancient monument.

St Patrick's Chapel, Peel

The Gatehouse, Peel Castle

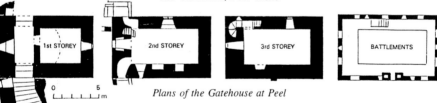

Plans of the Gatehouse at Peel

The curtain wall encloses a pear-shaped area nearly 200m long by 120m wide. Most of the circuit is about 5m high to the top of the parapet and is faced with huge grey slabs set on end to resemble huge boulders, i.e. it is not actually as strong and massive as it looks. On the east and SE the wall is earlier and of sandstone, and rises from closer to sea level, so of necessity it is slightly higher. The gatehouse is reached by steps from from the shore through an open porch. It measures 10.5m by 6.5m and contains three storeys, the lowest of which is divided into the entrance passage and a guardroom north of it, both parts being vaulted. The pleasant living room above is reached by a dog-leg passage in the SE corner from the porch wall-walk. The room was used by the constable and is now open to the sky. It has a fireplace in the east wall, windows to the east, west and south, and an access to curtain wall-walk formed out of what was once a latrine tucked under a stair in the SW corner. This stair leads to the topmost room, which has a fireplace on the east and modest window embrasures to the south and east, and then onto the wall-walk which has a parapet projected out on a single moulded corbelled course.

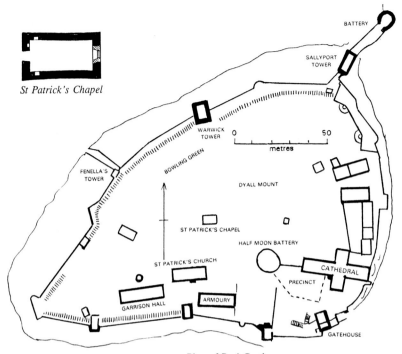

St Patrick's Chapel

Plan of Peel Castle

The Harbour Battery

Round Tower and garrison hall at Peel

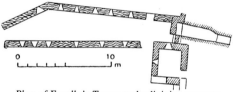

Plan of St Patrick's Church, Peel   *Plan of Fenella's Tower and adjoining passage*

The other towers on the circuit, all roofless, each contain two storeys of rooms. The rooms in the westernmost of the three towers on the south side are 6.6m long by 2.8m wide. The lowest room has a fireplace and a latrine but was poorly lighted. The walls facing the interior of the castle are just 0.9m thick, whilst the outer walls are 1.6m thick. The other two towers are similar except that they have walling of a more consistent thickness all round, and the easternmost tower, close to the gatehouse, is nearer to a square in plan and earlier, i.e. c1395. A loopholed 17th century wall runs towards the mid 16th century Half Moon Battery but does not join up with it, and a similar wall joins the battery to the cathedral west wall. The battery is a round of irregular shape varying from 12m to 13m in diameter externally. The battery has two gunports, one covering the harbour and the other Peel Hill. The armoury of the 1580s or 90s now lies in the line of fire of the latter. The armoury is a single storey building about 20m long standing complete except for its gables.

To the NW of the armoury is St Patrick's Church which is 19.5m long by 7.6m wide externally. As built in the 10th century it was only about 11.5m long and had antae or buttresses at the ends continuing the line of the side walls like many early churches in Ireland. Only the lowest courses remain of the work of this date, for it was rebuilt in the early 12th century, being lengthened slightly to the west and having courses of herringbone masonry on both the north and south sides. There is now a later medieval NW doorway but it appears that there was once a doorway in the west wall, which is now much reduced. A 17th century drawing shows a belfry for two bells upon this gable. The east end of the church, executed in grey slabs, is 15th century. No windows of this period remain in the side walls but there is a modest east window, originally of two or three lights. Outside the south wall is a stepped platform said to have been used by the sumner for making announcements.

The west end of Peel Castle

About 20m north of St Patrick's Church are remains of a small early chapel also dedicated to St Patrick. The side walls are low and bow inwards. The features comprise a west doorway, an east window, and three recesses. The round tower of the same period lies on the highest point of the island about 15m due west of St Patrick's Church. It measures 4.5m in external diameter above a plinth. The entrance doorway faces east towards the church and is 2.5m above the ground as a security measure. The tower is 15m high and has a corbelled parapet probably of the 1390s above four original openings facing the cardinal points. Between the tower and the rampart is a building 23m long by 6.2m wide internally which seems to have been a garrison hall or barracks. An old drawing shows a group of buildings to the west, now vanished, which formed a brew-house, kitchen and store serving it.

At the SW corner of the castle the lines of the northern and southern defences meet at an acute angle covered by a wide bastion which looks coeval with the walls, although it may be 16th century. From here the north wall runs to a triangular projection and then onto the Fenella Tower which is hardly more than a turret just 3.9m by 4.4m containing small rooms. The tower is named after a character in Sir Walter Scott's book Peveril of the Peak which places a dramatic incident in the story at this place. To the east of the tower is a postern through the rampart and curtain wall leading to an open passage 18m long to a cave on the shore. This passage was built during the Civil War and has musket loops on either side, plus doorways close to the castle outside wall. The Warwick Tower further to the east is the largest and most massive of all the towers but is no higher than the rest. It measures 12.2m by 9m over walls 2m thick and has round outer corners. The lower room has a fireplace but only one narrow south window. The upper storey has three openings, one now blocked. There is a latrine set in the parapet of the curtain on the east side of the tower. The tower is built of the same kind of masonry as the curtain but its awkward relationship to the latter suggests that it may be a generation or two earlier. The depressed area behind the rampart SW of this tower originally served as archery butts but in the 17th century was made into a bowling green. The featureless building at the SW end of this area seems to have been another chapel.

1st STOREY   2nd STOREY

Plans of Warwick Tower

0   5
metres

Plan of SW Tower

Warwick Tower

■ 14th Cent   ▤ 16th Cent
▧ 15th Cent   ▨ 17th Cent

Harbour Battery

0   5
└┴┴┴┴┘ m

Plan of Sallyport Tower and Harbour Battery

The Sallyport Tower projects far beyond the line of the curtain wall at the NE corner and probably predates it. A well lies within the rampart at this point. A stem of walling 3m across, pierced by a narrow passage, connects the tower to the main enceinte. The basement of the tower, which measures 6.4m wide by 13m long, contains a flight of steps down to a postern doorway with a drawbar slot. The northern half of the room above now contains toilets. The postern leads out into a 17th century open passage with loopholed sidewalls extending for 20m to connect with a round battery of c1548 covering the harbour. The battery measures 10m across over walling 2.6m thick and has, squeezed in under the low wall-walk, three gunports, two of them blocked by the 19th century breakwater and the third opened up as part of the path running round the exterior of the castle.

South of the Sallyport Tower is the battery of 1816-22, reused in the 1860s. The projection between it and the cathedral is a relic of the otherwise destroyed Galway (or Galloway?) Tower of the 1390s. This building collapsed or was dismantled by the the mid 15th century, and a block of that date now lies across where the west part of the tower would have been. This block runs at right angles to an early 15th century hall block orientated east-west, off which the tower chambers probably opened, the buttery and pantry being at the west end with a loft or musicians gallery above. This hall replaced a longer hall block of the 1390s parallel to it not far to the north, which was then subdivided and converted into kitchens, with ovens being inserted in the east wall. The older hall had an unusual layout with doors opposite each other in the middle of each side wall, and an extra door leading to the western half, which had a raised platform. The room must have had a mostly ceremonial purpose, and the small room projecting from the west end of the north side was probably a store for containing records or furnishings used in the ceremonies. At this time the castle was the administrative centre for the northern half of Man. However by the 15th century all these buildings were probably in use by a college of priests and the later block extending towards the cathedral must have been the dormitory of the "vicars choral", of which there were probably eight.

The domestic buildings at Peel Castle

When the Earls finally reclaimed the domestic buildings of the vicars choral for their own use in the early 17th century they made them more private by creating a small court bounded on the west by a wall linking the NE corner of the cathedral north transept with the SW corner of the new hall. By the 1660s large halls were out of fashion and the 15th century hall was divided into three compartments with a corridor along the south side at ground level, and a new floor was inserted to provide bedrooms above. The hall originally had a central open fireplace with the smoke rising to a louvre in the roof. When the building was subdivided a huge chimney was built over the site of the open fire but it took up too much space in the middle upper room, and so a new fireplace was created against the partition. Before long this in turn was replaced by a corner fireplace built against where the eastern partition met the north wall, blocking one of the original windows.

In the 1670s or 80s the former dormitory of the vicars' choral was subdivided to create a dining room with a drawing room beyond. The south end window was blocked by addition of a store and the walls were raised and a floor inserted to provide space for the earl's bedroom which was entered through inner and outer dressing rooms at the north end. These dressing rooms had fireplaces using the same flue as a new fireplace inserted in the dining room west wall. In their present ruined state all these rooms look very plain but an inventory of 1694 describes opulent furnishings, particularly in the main bedchamber where the bed had "gilt doves and claws with plaid hangings" and the walls were covered with "white, yellow and red flannel with six tapestries". In the court there was a seat in the NE corner and a lean-to passage or pentice ran down the east side to link the various rooms. At the south end was a well. The cobbling of the court between the hall block and the kitchen was executed by the mason Sam Green in 1702.

The ruined cathedral of St German is an impressive building, far larger and grander than any of the medieval parish churches on the Isle of Man, although modest in scale compared with the cathedrals and greater parish churches of England. It is a cruciform building 34.5m long internally, and 20.4m wide across the transepts, all four arms being about 6m wide. The finest part is the chancel of the 1230s built by Bishop Simon, whose tomb recess lies on the north side. The east end, rebuilt in modern times, has clasping pilaster buttresses on the corners and two more set between the three tall lancet windows. This wall now forms part of the precinct outer wall but until it collapsed in the 1660s or 70s there was a section of the sandstone curtain of 1393-9 enclosing this end. There are six lancets in each sidewall, again with tiny pilaster buttresses between them, and in the SE corner is a piscina. There are no certain remains of a supposed earlier church on this site and the tower, transepts and nave are essentially mid to late 13th century. The typically Early English style ornamentation of dog-tooth appears on the arch into the north transept. The arches are otherwise similar and of two chamfered orders. The nave has a plain north doorway with a draw-bar slot and two north lancets with trefoiled heads. The west window has a pair of pointed lights with a roundel above. The arcade alone remains of a former south aisle about 2.7m wide.

In the 1390s or the early 15th century the north transept was given a new east window and north doorway and the south transept seems to have been mostly rebuilt, being given buttresses on the east and south and a west doorway. A stair turret was built in the angle between this transept and the nave, the south aisle removed and its arcade blocked up. Since 1871 only one arch has remained blocked, with a window in it. Corbelled parapets and wall-walks were placed on the transepts and the heightened central tower. The pulpitum was moved from under the west tower arch to the east arch, and the choir stalls were moved from the crossing to the west bay of the chancel, their high backs necessitating the blocking of the westernmost lancets there. According to an account of 1692 there were eight of these stalls and there was an organ on a loft under the tower east arch. Under the tower is the tomb of Bishop Samuel Rutter, appointed 1661, who died in 1662.

St German's Cathedral, Peel, from the SW

St German's Cathedral, Peel, from the east

A new barrel vault with a series of thirteen closely spaced heavy ribs was erected in the 15th century over the crypt below the chancel. The crypt was originally quite low and the new vault, replacing an earlier one with a central pier, necessitated the raising of the chancel floor with a series of steps. The crypt is damp as a result of water oozing out of the rock at the west end and in later years formed a most unpleasant prison for those who broke the ecclesiastical laws. Few were kept here for more than a week but in 1662 the Quaker William Callow and a companion were confined in the crypt without heat or artificial light for sixteen days.

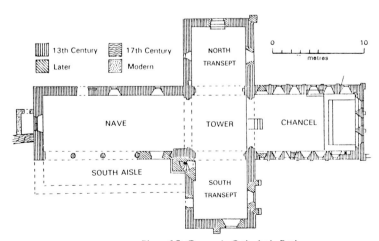

Plan of St German's Cathedral, Peel

ARTILLERY FORTS

BALLACHURRY FORT   SC 405970

Also known as Kerroogarroo, this fairly well preserved earthwork fort was erected c1645 on the orders of the 7th Earl of Derby to control the north end of Man. It has a low lying site and possibly once had a water filled moat. A rectangular court about 40m by 30m is enclosed by a rampart with a base width of about 17m rising up to 4m above the surrounding ditch. The outer edge of the ditch, now ill defined in places, formed a four pointed star so as to accommodate the diamond shaped bastions measuring 20m across on top placed at each of the corners.

CALF ISLAND   SC 167664 & 159647

The Calf of Man was garrisoned from the 1640s until at least 1713. Three Parliamentary ships which attacked the island in 1651 were successfully driven off. In 1694 the island was armed with three minions of iron and one of brass. By 1713 there were three additional guns. There are remains of batteries of this period overlooking the two landing points at Grant's Harbour and South Harbour.

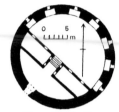

Plan of Derby Fort

Ballachurry Fort

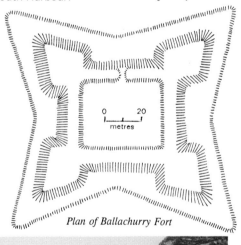

Plan of Ballachurry Fort

Derby Fort

DERBY FORT   SC 297675

This fort at the north end of St Michael's island commands the approach to the bay known as Derbyhaven and served as a lighthouse in the 18th century. At internal ground level seven evenly spaced gunports facing to seaward pierce a wall 2m thick rising 5.2m high externally to the top of the parapet protecting the wall-walk. Each merlon on the parapet contains two musket loops. The fort was built in the 1540s by Edward, 3rd Earl of Derby, but was remodelled a hundred years later by James, 7th Earl, his initials and the date 1645 appearing over the entrance doorway which faces SW. He also erected the now very faint earthworks on the landward or SW side of the fort. At that time the fort was armed with "one whole culvrain" and a "dem culvrain" firing 17lb and 4lb balls respectively. There are also traces of an earthwork covering the south end of the channel between the island and the Langness peninsular. By 1694 a barrack block had been built across the part of the interior nearest the entrance of the stone fort, blocking one of the gunports, and in 1695 a battery was built on the tip of the Ronaldsway peninsular, traces of it having been revealed by excavation. Further works were deemed necessary in this area in 1713, when four brass drakes were mounted on Hango Hill, and another battery armed with an iron minion erected at Claberry, south of where the golf club house is towards the north end of the SE side of the Langness peninsular. These three sites were all abandoned by the early 18th century.

DOUGLAS FORT   SC 386754

The name Fort Street is the only reminder of a circular fort assumed to have been built in the 1540s by the 3rd Earl of Derby and demolished in 1818. For some years before then it had served as a prison. The building seems to have had two storeys, the uppermost of which would have had a fireplace and would have been the guardroom when prisoners were kept below. A plan of 1758 indicates the building measured about 14.3m in diameter over walls 2.4m thick and probably about 6m high to the top of the parapet. The fort was armed with "four pieces" of cannon in the 1640s. The "new fort of Douglas" built in 1666-7 seems to have been a gun platform on the rocks to seaward. The platform seems to have been enlarged in 1690-1 and in 1758 measured about 15m by 14m with a curved front to seaward. An inventory of 1713 mentions two demi-culverins and a minion on the platform, two minions in the "middle room", probably the upper storey of the fort, and a saker, a minion and a small mortar "in the platform above", probably the roof.

RAMSEY FORT AND BATTERIES   SC 472932 & 454946, etc

Fear of piracy on the one hand and Parliamentary invasion on the other led to a number of batteries being set up by the 7th Earl of Derby in the 1640s to guard the 2km long beach between the mouth of the Sulby River and the headland at Gob ny Rona. Slight overgrown earthworks remain of a battery on Gob ny Rona, but the sea has destroyed the site of the Dane's Fort just north of the mouth of the Ballure stream and nothing remains of the fort by the mouth of the Sulby River. The Dane's Fort had two sakers in 1694. The fort at Gob ny Rona, also called Port Lewaigue, was given a new plarform in 1693 and was then armed with a demi-culverin and a saker. This site was reoccupied in 1782. The Ramsey fort is said to have been a round blockhouse. A new platform seems to have been built alongside it in 1693 for mounting a culverin and two sakers. By the 1740s it was in a ruinous state but it was remodelled as a combined fort and prison in 1757, only to be sold to a merchant at the Revestment a few years later.

RELIGIOUS HOUSES

BEMAKEN FRIARY   SC 250703

An outbuilding of a farm just south of Ballabeg in the parish of Arbory is the much altered 14th century church of a Franciscan friary founded in 1373 by William Montague, Earl of Salisbury. The building has a blocked east window and contains several openings with shouldered lintels of the so-called Caernarvon arch type. The twelve original friars came from Ireland. The friary was dissolved in 1540. Celtic ogham gravestones of the 5th or 6th century have been found here.

MIRESCOGH   SC 404952

This was a originally a cell of the Cistercian Abbey of Rievaulx in Yorkshire but was later handed over to Rushen Abbey. No remains survive but it is thought to have stood upon what is now the farm of Ballamona in the parish of Lezayre.

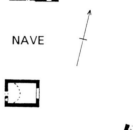

NAVE

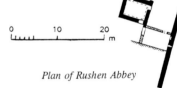

0   10   20
m

Plan of Rushen Abbey

The Tower of Rushen Abbey Church

Dovecote Tower, Rushen Abbey

Former Church of Bemaken Friary

RUSHEN ABBEY   SC 277702

A few fragments of the abbey of St Mary lie in the neglected garden of a hotel on the west side of Ballasalla. King Olaf I gave land for founding the abbey in 1134. It was a daughter house of Furness in Lancashire and like that house was originally Savignac but became Cistercian in 1147. On the north side of the church is a tower, thought to be 15th century but containing a blocked round 12th or 13th century east arch. An overgrown vault remains south of where the south transept would have been. Further east is a tower-like building containing nesting boxes for pigeons and adjoining the remains of the guest house and abbot's quarters. The abbey was dissolved in 1540 and the buildings passed to the Lord of Man. Bishop Bridgman purchased the site from Deemster Moore in the 1670s with the intention of founding a school or university. This plan failed and Moore repurchased the site and built a house from materials taken from the ruins, now the core of the hotel. Not far north of the abbey is the delightful packhorse bridge of Crossag.

ST BRIDGET'S NUNNERY   SC 373753

This may have been the nunnery in Douglas where Robert Bruce stayed in 1313. At the dissolution the Abbess, Margaret Goodman, and three nuns were expelled and the lands reverted to the Earl of Derby, who sold them to his Receiver Robert Calcott, who then married the former abbess. They built a new house but it was replaced by one higher up the hill in 1830. The nunnery chapel still survives and was long used as a coach house. It is a plain rectangle with restored windows, a doorway on the south and a tomb recess on the north next to a reset holy water stoup once by the doorway. A rood screen has now been inserted.

GAZETTEER OF MANX CHURCHES

ANDREAS *St Andrew* SC 405993

The present church is a very wide 19th century building and has a detached tower dated 1869 with a path through its base since there are archways in the east and west walls. The tower is a renewal of an original which formed a noted landmark in the northern plain. The collection of seven cross-slabs inside the church includes one dating from the 10th century erected by Sandulf The Black to his wife Arinbjorg and having animals on both sides. Another depicts a scene from the Norse pagan mythological battle of Ragnarck, and others show the legendry hero Sigurd roasting a dragon's heart and his foster brother Gunnar being fatally bitten in a snake pit.

ARBORY *St Columba* SC 247706

The parish takes its name from the original dedication of the church to St Caerbrie of Coleraine. The date 1757 appears below the east window, an unusual position for a datestone, and the building is probably a rebuild of a generation or two later with the usual long series of round arched windows. The west tower is 20th century. Of greater interest is the monument inside to Captain John Quilliam, a hero of the naval battles of Copenhagen and Trafalgar, being quartermaster of the Victory at the latter battle. From the proceeds of his share of prize money won at sea he bought the estate of Ballakeighan and became a member of the House of Keys.

BALLAUGH *St Mary* SC 341958

The village lies at a crossroads on the Peel to Ramsey road and there is situated the present church of 1832. The old church lies in trees 2.5km to the north. It is first mentioned in a Papal Bull of 1231. In 1717 the church was lengthened eastward partly at the expense of Bishop Wilson, and the west end was then remodelled with twin pilasters supporting an octagonal bellcote. The vaulted west porch is of the same period but the inner doorway may be medieval. The three windows in each side wall are probably of 1757-77 when rear and side galleries were added with access steps beside the porch, providing seating in all for 300 people. The medieval font is set into the SW window embrasure. By the time the much larger new church was built in the village, the old church was in a decayed state and it remained thus until 1849 when the then rector had the building reduced to its original length and re-roofed. In the church is a fine 10th century cross-slab with a runic inscription recording that it was erected by Aleif Ljotolfsson in memory of his son Ulf.

Porch of Ballaugh Church

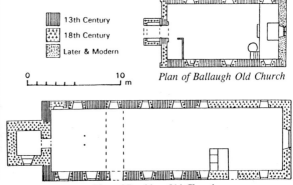

▦ 13th Century
▨ 18th Century
▨ Later & Modern

0   10 m

Plan of Ballaugh Old Church

Plan of Braddan Old Church

Braddan Old Church

BRADDAN   *St Brendan*   SC 364768

Some walling in the old church may go back beyond 1291 when Bishop Mark held a synod here, and the finial cross on the east gable is probably 12th century. Bishop Wilson recorded that in 1704 the church was rendered, given a new flagged floor and a new east window. At that time the church had a double bellcote. A gallery was erected c1740 to increase the seating space as the building then still served the town of Douglas which had only a modest chapel-of-ease. In the 1770s the building was lengthened both to east and west and provided with a tower with an unusual open top stage and a double bellcote on the east side. Bricks on the back of the bellcote form the date 1774. As remodelled the main body of the church has six round headed windows on the south side and two doorways, that in the nave being wider and having a niche for a lost date-stone above it. There were originally seven windows in the north wall but one near the east end was blocked up when one of a pair of 19th century monuments to the Murray family was placed against it. The safe dated 1817 in the vestry in the base of the tower was provided as the result of a theft of money for the poor the previous year. In the nave are a collection of ten cross-slabs, the best known being that with a runic inscription reading "Thorleif Hnakki erected this cross to the memory of Fiaco his son, the nephew of Eabor". The font lies set in the wall at the NW corner and there is a plain three-decker pulpit of the 1770s on the south side. Close by the to north of the old church is a much larger new church which was consecrated in August 1876.

BRIDE   *St Bridget*   NX 449012

The old church was demolished in 1869 and replaced by a new church alongside to a design by Ewan Christian. It is a wide building in a Lombardic style with an east apse and a porch-tower on the south side dated 1875, but bearing a reset sundial of 1824. In the porch are the old font and stoup. Three cross-slabs are displayed in the SW corner of the nave. One has a ring-chain ornament and a runic inscription on the edge telling us the cross was raised by Dugald in memory of his wife Cathmaoill. Another, now fragmentary, is an altar front from the keeill site at Ballavarkish.

CASTLETOWN   *St Mary*   SC 265674

In the early 13th century a chapel was built to serve the settlement growing up near Castle Rushen. Either as an original feature or as the result of an early alteration it was given a south aisle with an arcade of three round arches on square piers with the corners chamfered off. The east wall was rebuilt in the late medieval period. After a new church was built the chapel of St Mary was converted into a school as part of Bishop Wilson's programme of encouraging education for all. The aisle was demolished and two arches blocked, but the east arch was kept open to give onto a new transeptal school-room. The north wall was also remodelled then whilst the east and west walls were given new windows in the 19th century. The building ceased to be a school in 1930 and it now forms a tourist information office.

DOUGLAS   *St George*   SC 378755

Douglas lies in what was originally part of the parish of Braddon and had no church of its own until 1641, when a small chapel of St Mary was erected close to where the Saddle Hotel now stands on North Quay. With the growth of the town it quickly became inadequate and with Bishop Wilson's encouragement a larger chapel dedicated to St Matthew was built in 1708 on the side of the present cast-iron market hall on North Quay. At a meeting in the assembly Rooms in 1761 it was resolved to build a new and much larger chapel and work was soon begun on the present building. By 1766 the funds collected by the trustees ran out and the building remained incomplete until further funds were raised in 1776, the church finally being completed in November 1780, and being consecrated in September 1781. The building has aisles with galleries supported by fluted columns of wood and there are consequently two levels of windows. At the west end is an embattled tower with its base serving as the porch and being flanked by vestries. In 1864 the original apse was taken down and the chancel lengthened, being flanked by a vestry and organ chamber. The organ was purchased in 1788 from the Musical Academy in Dublin and was used by Handel there for a rendition of the Messiah in 1742. It has subsequently been much rebuilt and altered. In 1877 St George's was raised from the status of a chapel-of-ease to Braddan to being a parish church in its own right.

St George's Church, Douglas

St Patrick's Chapel, Jurby

JURBY   *St Patrick*   SC 349985 & 346982

Sketch of lost old church, Lezayre

The present parish church is a white-washed 19th century building. It contains five cross-slabs, one of which has a figure depicting Heimdall, Warder of the Gods, blowing his horn to summon the gods to the mythological battle of Ragnarok.

In a field 0.4km SW of the parish church is a ruined chapel, also apparently dedicated to St Patrick. It is similar in size to the early keeills but has mortared masonry and a small plain mullioned east window, the doorway being on the north side. The west end has a fireplace flanked by recesses so in later years the building must have been used as a dwelling. It contains a fragment of a cross-slab.

LEZAYRE   *Christchurch*   SC 424942

The present church completed in 1835 to a design by John Welch has a west tower rising above the surrounding trees. A plaque marks the site of the original church higher up the hillside to the south. It was dedicated to Holy Trinity or Kirk Christ and was rebuilt in 1704. In the porch formed in the tower base of the new church are the old font and stoup recovered from Glen Auldyn after a flood in 1931, fragments of several cross-slabs, an inscription recording the rebuilding of the north wall and roof of the old church in 1760, and a tombstone of Deemster John Curghey of Ballakillingan from the chancel of the old church.

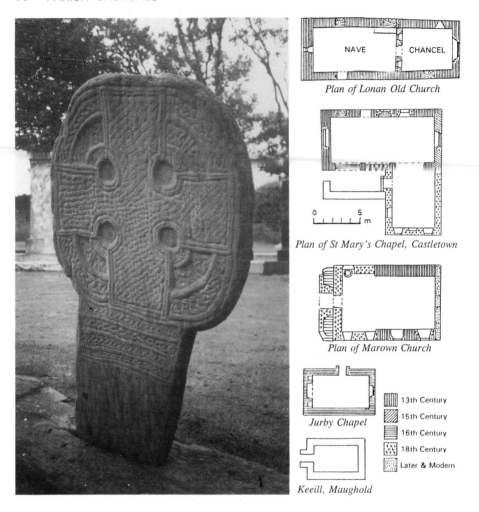

Plan of Lonan Old Church

Plan of St Mary's Chapel, Castletown

Plan of Marown Church

Jurby Chapel

	13th Century
	15th Century
	16th Century
	18th Century
	Later & Modern

Keeill, Maughold

LONAN   *St Adamnan*   SC 427794

The old church lies far from any centre of population and was superseded in 1833 by a new church of All Saints built at Boilley Veen. The new church also lies alone but is more convenient, being between the villages of Laxey and Baldrine. The old church has a roofless nave with masonry probably of 12th century date with little mortar. The blocked north doorway and the rectangular west window may be original. The pointed headed south doorway is 13th or 14th century. Of the early 13th century is the chancel with one original north window which was re-opened when this part of the building was re-roofed and given a new east window and a west wall containing a doorway in 1895-7. There are traces of what appears to have been an original priest's doorway on the south side. South of the church is a very fine cross-slab still in its original socket stone, whilst there is a collection of other cross-slabs in a shed built to cover them in the NW corner of the churchyard

Lonan Old Church

MALEW   *St Lua (or Molua)*   SC 246705

This white-washed building lies alone 2km north of Castletown. The irregular shape of the walling at the west end suggests that some medieval work has survived subsequent rebuildings which have given the church a north transept and a separate, narrower, chancel. The double bellcote and west doorway may be ancient. On the SE corner of the nave is a D-shaped stone bearing an incised cross, probably a consecration mark. The church is first recorded in a Papal bull of 1153. In the nave was buried William Christian, better known as Illiam Dhone, Governor of Man 1656-8, executed at Hangohill on a charge of rebellion in 1663 by the Earl of Derby.

Malew Church

Marown Old Church　　　　*Cross-slab at Marown*

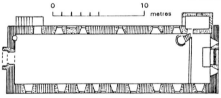

Plan of Maughold Church

MAROWN *St Runius* SC 312787　　*Dog-tooth ornament on doorway at Maughold*

The present parish church beside the Douglas to St John's road was begun in 1849 and the old church on the hill to the south then became just a mortuary chapel. The eastern half of the building was demolished and the gap closed with a thin wall pierced by a doorway through which coffins could be carried. This doorway was closed up in 1906. The original church had a doorway on the south side, traces of which can be seen under the second window from the east. In the 1750s the church was lengthened with thinner walling to the west and given a new west doorway with a vaulted porch flanked by external stairs to a west gallery removed a hundred years later. The jambs of the west doorway are clearly medieval work and they are likely to have come from the ruined chapel of St Trinian 1.6km to the north. The large font, taken outside the church in the 1750s, has been set into the recess of a NW window of the 1750s, blocked in 1906. Near it is a stoup, latterly used as a font. There are three early cross-slabs by the present east wall.

Maughold Church

MAUGHOLD   *St Maughold*   SC 494917

By the 7th century a Celtic monastery was flourishing on this site. The church has been developed from an early keeill and four others are known to have existed in the churchyard. The lower parts of three of them, referred to as north, middle, and east, still remain and the fourth, west, stood where there is a short granite pillar 9m NW of the church porch. The north keeill is the smallest and has well built dry-stone walls and a west doorway flanked by short wall stubs to form a tiny porch. It now has a cobble floor. The middle keeill has a west doorway set off-centre towards the south. The east keeill is more thinly walled and has a well shaft of later date lying where its SE corner would have been. One of the 46 cross-slabs collected together under a shelter south of the church has an inscription referring to the provision of a water supply for the monastery which could be this well. A stone commemorating the 7th century monastic-bishop Irneit is the oldest Cross-slab on Man. Another, erected by Hedin in memory of his daughter Hlif, has a picture of a Viking ship.

The church itself forms a plain rectangle except for a tiny Victorian vestry at the NE corner. The nave is probably 12th century, the likely age of the large font in the NW corner, whilst the east end is a 13th century extension. Remains of two small lancets were revealed in the south wall during rebuilding in 1860 and were restored in 1901, and there are two more in the east wall with a Victorian window between them. There are traces of a north doorway, probably also 13th century. Further west is a much later upper doorway serving the west gallery. Over the outer arch of the shallow west porch is a reset section of 13th century dog-tooth ornamentation. The 14th century parish cross, the only one of its type left on the island, originally stood on the green west of the church. In 1937 it was placed in front of the cross shelter until 1989, when, after being restored at the Manx Museum, it was placed inside the church to save it from the elements. The east face depicts the crucifixion, the west the Virgin and Child, the south a kneeling knight, and the north a shield with an oak-leaved rose. One of the shields on the neck shows the Three Legs of Man.

Middle Keeill, Maughold

MICHAEL   *St Michael*   SC 317908

The tomb of the celebrated Bishop Wilson (in office from 1698 until his death in 1755) lies close to a small fragment of the walling of the chancel of the old church in the NE corner of the churchyard. The fragment has a jamb of an 18th century window and bears a tablet stating that this part was rebuilt in 1776 by Dr Thomas Wilson, a son of the bishop. The old church is said to have had a west tower. The present cruciform church with a high west tower with corner turrets with pinnacles was begun in 1834. On display now in the north transept, but formerly in the unusually large lych gate erected to shelter them in 1907, is a collection of cross-slabs from the 7th to the 11th centuries. One of them has a runic inscription indicating that it was one of a large number of crosses carved by Gaut Bornson in the mid 10th century. The largest of the collection is that erected by Joalf to his mother Frida. One cross depicts a crucifixion scene and another has a dragon on each side. In 1972 a hoard of coins dating from the 1060s was discovered during the digging of a grave in the churchyard. There were coins of Norman, Hiberno-Norse and Anglo Saxon origin, plus others probably minted in that century on the Isle of Man. Another hoard of about the same date was discovered while digging out the foundations of the old church in 1834.

Fragment of old church in front of new church at Kirkmichael

ONCHAN   *St Peter*   SC 400782

It seems that the church was originally dedicated to St Conchem, the Irish equivalent of St Christopher. Captain Bligh of the Bounty was married here in 1781. The church was entirely rebuilt in the 19th century but in the porch in the base of the west tower are fragments of six cross-slabs and a cross formerly on the gable of the original 12th century building. One slab has the name of the carver Thorid.

PATRICK   *Holy Trinity*   SC 245822

The present church of 1881 has replaced a building erected in 1714 of which foundations are said to survive under the long grass in the older graveyard to the north. This building had a wing or transept on one side and was probably once dedicated to St Patrick. Archdeacon Moore described it thus: "The parish church is damp and unhealthy. The walls are not exactly perpendicular and in the days of Judaism would have been pronounced leprous. The roof is bad, there is no spouting, and the windows are very much decayed". The original parish church is that lying close to the round tower in the precinct of Peel Castle, a rather inconvenient position.

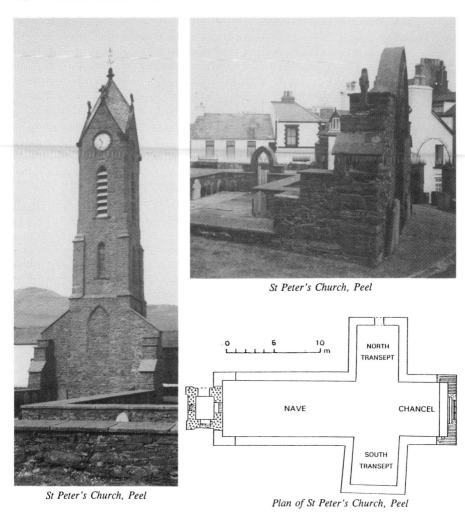

St Peter's Church, Peel

St Peter's Church, Peel

Plan of St Peter's Church, Peel

PEEL   *St Peter*   SC 243842

In the middle of the town are ruins of a cruciform church built in 1551 as a chapel-of-ease to the cathedral of St German on St Patrick's Island, by then enclosed by the walls of Peel Castle and in any case difficult of access for the townsfolk. The church was later raised to full parochial status but was abandoned in favour of the new church further east erected in 1884 with funds collected by Bishop Rowley Hill for a projected restoration of the cathedral. The new church originally had a spire but it was dismantled after being damaged by a storm in 1907. Most of the old church only stands about waist high and few details are preserved. There is a piscina in the chancel south wall and the east wall stands complete with a 19th century traceried window. The only other part now standing high is the lofty 17th century west tower. The south transept is irregularly set out and inclines to the west.

Kirk Christ, Rushen

RAMSEY   *St Catherine*   SC 456937   *St Paul*   SC 454944

The tiny chapel at Ballure is an ancient keeill rebuilt in 1850 and then dedicated to St Catherine, the original dedication being unknown. Ramsey lay in the parish of Maughold and was only provided with a church when St Paul's was built in 1822. A tablet on the buildings tells us it was enlarged in 1844, improved in 1924 and given a new west porch in 1937. The church is a cruciform building with an east apse and a west tower. It is whitewashed with pink dressings. The windows are vaguely gothic in style except for the round arched ones of the porch.

RUSHEN   *Holy Trinity*   SC 208694

Known as Kirk Christ, this is a white-washed rectangular building of the 18th and 19th centuries with round arched windows, bullet shaped corner pinnacles, an east apse, a west gallery, and an octagonal bell turret.

SANTON   *St Sanctain*   SC 310712

The church is a whitewashed rectangle with corner pinnacles. According to the registers the north side of the church was rebuilt in 1703 and the south side in 1715, whilst the bellcote was added in 1725, so no medieval work survives. There seems to have been some rebuilding in 1774 and the west gallery is of 1785. Upon it are fixed the Royal Arms of William IV. There are two cross slabs in the church and also a Roman tombstone to one Avitus. The great stone west of the church marks the grave of the Cosnahan family, several of whom were vicars of Santon.

Santon Church

St Trinian's Chapel

ST MICHAEL'S   *St Michael*   SC 295675

This 12th century chapel on St Michael's Island at the entrance to Derby Haven is a ruin but with the masonry fairly intact. It has a round arched south doorway. There are small original windows in the east wall and in the east end of each side wall, plus another high up in the west wall, beneath a pointed bellcote perhaps of later date.

ST TRINIAN'S   *St Trinian*   SC 318803

In a field above the Douglas to St John's road are ruins of a chapel on the site of a keill. Two early crosses found inside the church are 6th or 7th century. The north wall contains two Norman windows and other reset features of that period, including half of an arch or two orders, either a doorway or former chancel arch. The chapel was lengthened to the east in the 14th century, the east window, the SE window, the priest's doorway on the north, and the main south doorway all being of that date. The stones of the main doorway are said to have been reset at Marown old church.

St Michael's Chapel

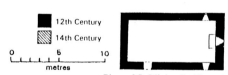

Plan of St Michael's Chapel

Plan of St Trinian's Chapel